2010

Dr. Jeffery L. Walker

Dr. Hallie R. Harper

African American Males Why Are You So Angry?

I CAN'T DO THIS ANY MORE! I'M GETTING READY TO HANDLE THIS!!!!

The Anger Management

Workbook For

African American Males

Acknowledgments

This workbook was developed to assist the African American male with the transformation of going from angry to anger management, by using the Stop-Drop and Walk format. The workbook was written by Jeffery L. Walker Ed.D and Hallie R. Harper Ed.D.

Dedication

This workbook is dedicated to all the African American recipients who are and were exposed to the ramifications of out of control anger.

Electronic Access

This workbook can be ordered online at www.ptceiandrise.org

CONTENTS

INTRODUCTION

This workbook is tailored to assist African American males in alleviating or mitigating their internal conflict, which derives from their inability to understand their cultural stressors such as; geographical location, economic resources, educational advancement, relationships, family issues, racism and discrimination.

The stressors and strains that African American males endure are different from other cultures, for example; being born African American can be (but does not have to be) hazardous to one's mental health, by suppressing their stressors which can block their ability to become a fully functioning human being.

The STOP DROP and WALK 8 week program provides African American males with the necessary tools to combat their internal conflict. In using this workbook African American males can develop skills that will allow them to navigate through their environmental and social turbulence.

Orientation: Week 1

Overview of the STOP DROP and WALK Principles of Anger Management

In this first group, you will receive an overview of the STOP DROP and Walk Principles of Anger Management. This includes the purpose of the group, criteria for the group, definitions of terms, rewards and consequences, contributing factors to anger, the physical and cognitive signs of anger, anger journal, feeling chart and self-knowledge.

I.   **Purpose of the Group:**
   A) Acknowledge your anger
   N) Notice your underlining feelings of anger
   G) Get in touch with your
   E) Entire gamut of emotions
   R) Release your anger as soon as possible

II.   **Criteria for the Group:**

1) *Group Safety: No violence or threats of violence toward staff or other group members are allowed at any time. It is important that everyone is able to view the group as a safe place to express feelings and experiences without fear of verbal or physical abuse.*

2) *Confidentiality: Group members should not discuss outside of the group what other members say.*

3) *Take Home Assignments: Brief homework assignments will be given each week. Doing these assignments will allow for and foster growth toward improving your anger management skills.*

4) *Absences and Cancellations: Participants must be willing to sign a written agreement acknowledging an understanding that group participation is mandatory.* **Participants can not miss any portion of the program unless prior approval is agreed upon.**

5) *Anger Reduction Plan/Melt Down System:*
   • *Acknowledge who or what you're angry at*
   • *Find a quiet place to sit or lay down*

• *Take 3 deep breaths*
• *Talk to someone about your anger*

III.   Definitions Of : A A R R:

The anger stimulus is different in the African American males than in other minority and non-minority groups. Although the anger stimulus is similar in other minority groups it is not the same because the anger factors have a deeper psychological and sociological component.

Anger: *Occurs when an individual cannot manipulate the stimulus response of another individual. For example; a mother tells her son to empty the trash before she comes home from work, however the trash has not been emptied when she gets home. The mother becomes angry because she could not control the situation.*

Aggression: *Can be intimidating or cause bodily harm to another person. Aggression has an emotional cousin which is **passive-aggressive behavior.** This is when another individual is mad at you and you're not around, they may do something that indirectly affects or hurts you.*

Resentment: *This occurs when an individual displays **passive behavior;** they do nothing but simmer when they're upset or angry at another individual.*

Rage: *This consists of two components' **cognitive movement** occurs when an individual is thinking about what they are going to do to someone if they don't stop bothering them.* **Physical Altercation:** occurs when an individual can no longer tolerate the behavior by the opposition and explode into temporary insanity, in which has a duration of 7seconds. Immediately after the physical altercation phase the individual will experience the **"quiet storm phase".** This phase is where the individual becomes shame based and needs 50 feet to gather their thoughts about what just happened.

Given the four definitions of A A R R, what thoughts and concerns do you have? Please explain:

Anger: _____

Aggression: _____

Resentment: _____

Rage: _____

IV: **The Physical/Cognitive Signs of Anger:**

- Get in someone's face

- Shoving, grabbing, hitting

- Break something

- Call someone names

- Give someone a dirty look

- Silent treatment

- Spread rumors

- Get others to "gang up"

List some additional ways anger maybe affecting you:

_____

_____

_____

_____

_____

_____

V: Psychosocial Triggers:

Besides the physical signs that we sense in our body that alerts us to feeling angry there are other signs, called triggers, that we can learn to understand in order to take charge of our anger.

There are two types of triggers, external and internal:

*External: these are the things that are done to us. Like someone lying or putting you down.

*Internal: these are the messages we give ourselves, called self-talk, that gets us all worked up. Sometimes it is based on assumptions or incorrect information.

VI: Rewards and Consequences:

The expression of anger can be a positive process if it is released in a non-confrontational manner. By using the "Melt Down System" which allows an individual to convey their anger in a safe and non-threatening manner. Inappropriate expressions of anger can result in negative consequences such as; physical harm, incarceration, and possible loss of life can occur.

List some rewards to using anger appropriately.

_____
_____
_____
_____
_____

List some negative consequences you have experienced when expressing anger inappropriately.

_____
_____
_____
_____
_____

VI: Contributing Factors to Anger:

Geographical Location: Most African Americans are victims of social deprivation primarily because of their pigmentation. This type of discrimination can cause a unique stressor that can develop into emotional turbulence. African Americans do not have the same geographical freedom as Caucasians to live where they choose without social consequences. This form of geographical prejudice has a direct effect to the "**angry black male**" syndrome.

Economic Resources: Many African American males derive from a single-parent home where the mother is the head of the household. The father is missing therefore economic resources are limited. This creates a survival oriented environment which can produce anger if there is no opportunity for economic growth.

Educational Advancement: African American males are not unaware of the importance of educational advancement, but may suffer from cultural mistrust, which is a significant predictor of academic achievement. As African American males mistrust increases, their academic expectations decrease, as mistrust increase so does their oppositional attitudes. African American males are an endangered species in and out of the school system. Statistics show that African American males are more prone to drop out of high school than any other ethnic group. The question is why? We need to examine the stressors that seem to overpower African American males, which force them to drop out of school and pursue a career in the criminal justice system (jail).

Relationships: African American males do not hold their respected place in relationships today for reasons that go very deep. It must be a place where each individual regards the other person's rights and feelings as they would their own. This is a crucial element that is missing in the majority of African American relationships. African American males have trouble bonding because they don't have the opportunity to see their parents bond. Many grow up like a flower deprived of sunshine and water. Some are robbed of spiritual, psychological, emotional and intellectual growth because the father is not there to give the male parental instruction. Without this vital instruction the young African American male has nothing to mimic from. Bonding is paramount in any relationship. When African American males miss watching their parents bond, they learn to hide their feelings and that can cause serious stress in the relationship that ultimately creates conflict that produces anger.

Family Issues*: African American fathers are missing in the African American family system; tradition now holds the black female as head of the household. Missing are the African American male as role models, leaders, and most importantly men who need to* ***"show up"*** *in the black family. When they are missing from the family young males tend to search for a sense of belonging in the wrong places. This may explain why so many African American males are gravitating towards gangs hoping to receive acceptance and love; instead they receive a constant dose of anger because of the life style that they choose.*

Racism and Discrimination: *The historical roots of the African American male is quite significant because it reflects an important social group transformation and reality in terms of group identity, social opportunities, life chances, life styles and discriminatory behaviors. Racism is the greatest causation for anger in the African American community. Many African American males feel like their living beneath the floor boards of society; listening to the dominant culture. Many feel that no matter what they do in this society, they will always be an invisible species. This type of mindset is anger producing, which can result in self-defeating behavior.*

These are some of the crippling factors that affect African American males. These factors have a vital effect on the development of the African American male. They shape their cultural values, which directly affect the way they view themselves and others. African American males need not wait for the 'storm to pass they need to learn how to dance in the rain'.

Anger Journal

WHAT: What am I angry about? Find your source:

_____

_____

_____

_____

WHO: Who am I angry at? Find your target:

_____

_____

_____

_____

WHEN: When was I angry? Give the date and time:

_____

_____

_____

_____

WHERE: Where did it occur? School, home, social setting etc…:

_____

_____

_____

_____

HOW: How did you resolve it? What was the outcome?

_____

_____

_____

_____

FEELINGS CHART

Which anger style do you have?

SEVEN TOWERS OF ANGER STYLES:

BLAMER: *This anger style thinks it is someone else's fault.*

EXPLODER: *This anger style loses their temper and starts yelling, throwing things, hitting*

and so on.

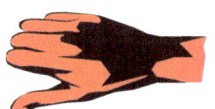

PUT DOWNER: *Gets nasty saying sarcastic or hurtful thing.*

STUFFER: *Holds everything in and pretends like nothing is wrong.*

TRIANGULATOR: *Gossips and sucks other people into the conflict, trying to get someone to take his or her side.*

WITHDRAWER: *Pulls out of the situation and quits talking to the person they are angry at.*

PROBLEM SOLVER: *Can admit when they are wrong and feels the need to fix everyone's situation.*

ANGER-RESENTMENT-RAGE EXPLODE METER

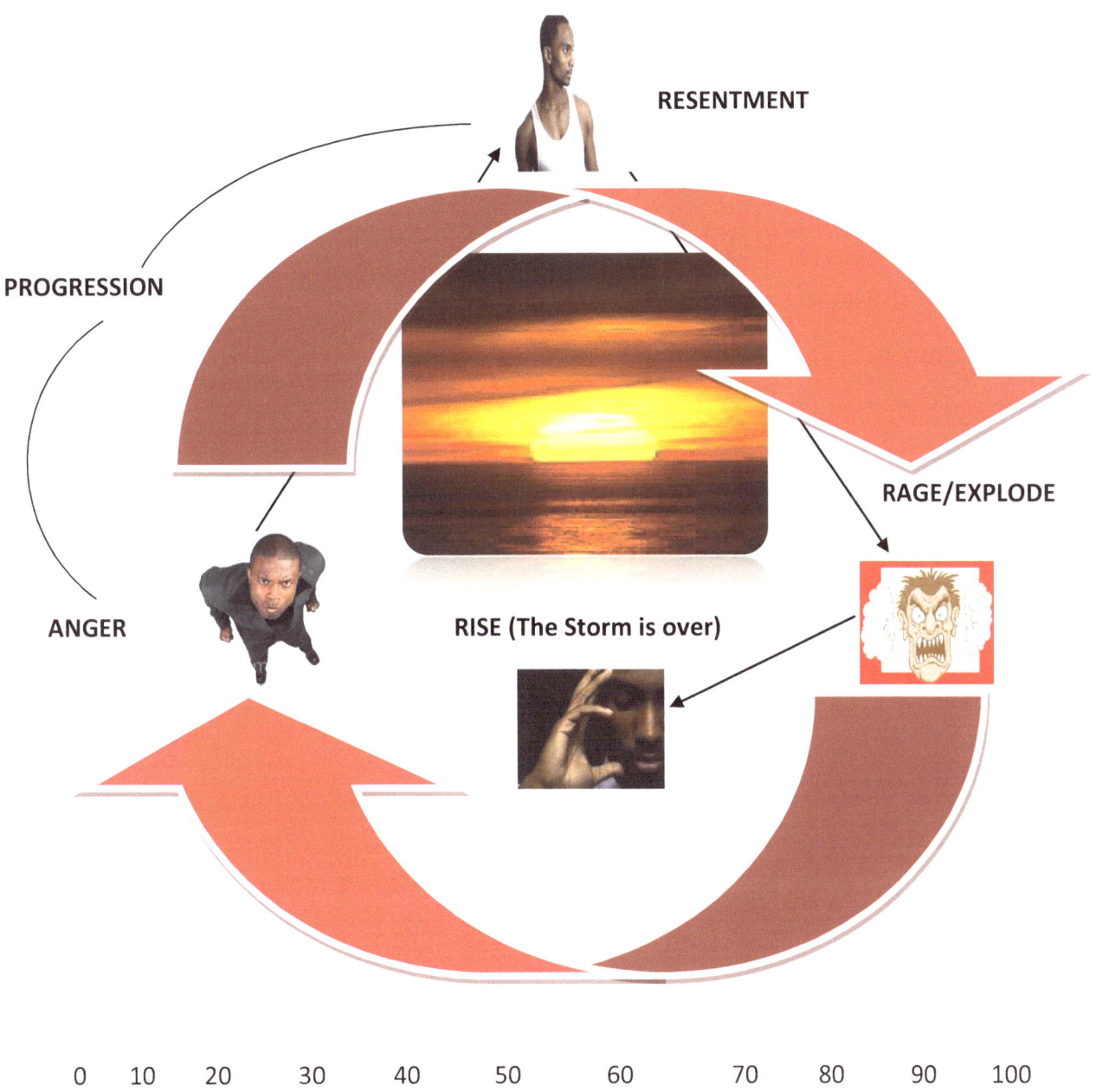

RESENTMENT

PROGRESSION

RAGE/EXPLODE

ANGER

RISE (The Storm is over)

0   10   20   30   40   50   60   70   80   90   100

When anger is not expressed appropriately unresolved anger turns into resentment unresolved resentment turns into rage, which has two components. Component A: Cognitive Movement and Component B: Physical Altercation. When these two components interchange with each other temporary insanity can occur. After this phase you will experience the quiet storm. Here is where you collect your thoughts and examine your behavior.

Where are you on this meter? Chart where you are on a weekly basis.

WEEK 1

Anger: Why?

_____

_____

Resentment: Why?

_____

_____

Rage: Why?

_____

_____

Explode: Why?

_____

_____

RISE: Why?

_____

_____

SELF KNOWLEDGE:

What did you learn from this step?

_____
_____
_____
_____
_____
_____
_____
_____
_____
_____
_____
_____
_____
_____
_____
_____
_____
_____
_____
_____
_____
_____
_____
_____
_____
_____
_____
_____
_____

Week 2

Stopping the Manifestation of Anger

In this step you will learn how to stop the manifestation of anger. You will learn to identify physical signs of anger and the cognitive cues that provoke anger outbursts.

I. **The Four Skills to Identifying Anger**
    - Determine why I am angry
    - Determine who or what I am angry toward
    - Look at the situation and define the problem
    - Is this something I can change?

What am I angry about?

_____

_____

_____

_____

Who or what is the source of my anger?

_____

_____

_____

_____

What happened to make me angry?

_____

_____

_____

_____

What can I do about it?

_____

_____

_____

_____

II.   Psychosocial Cues to Anger

When you experience anger it is important to be able to identify the cues that cause anger. These cues are warning signs that you are becoming angry. When you are becoming angry remember these cues; Thoughts, Feelings and Behaviors.

When you experience anger write down your TFB's.

Thoughts or cognitive cues: what are you thinking about when you are angry?

_____

_____

_____

_____

Feeling cues: what emotions do you experience when you are angry?

_____

_____

_____

_____

Behavior cues: what do you do when you are angry?

_____

_____

_____

_____

III.   Mapping Out Your Anger

In this section you began the process of mapping out your anger, identifying and understanding your emotional and cognitive cues that produced negative behaviors.

Go back and look at your answers in the previous section if anything has changed write the changes down and record them on your TFB chart.

T) Thoughts: what thoughts do I currently have when thinking about anger?

_____

_____

_____

_____

F) Feelings: What emotions am I currently experiencing?

_____

_____

_____

_____

B): Behaviors: what do I do when angry according to the six towers of anger?

_____

_____

_____

_____

Do I agree with my anger style, why or why not?

_____

_____

_____

_____

T.F.B. CHART

THOUGHTS	FEELINGS	BEHAVIORS
_____	_____	_____
_____	_____	_____
_____	_____	_____
_____	_____	_____
_____	_____	_____
_____	_____	_____
_____	_____	_____
_____	_____	_____
_____	_____	_____
_____	_____	_____
_____	_____	_____
_____	_____	_____
_____	_____	_____
_____	_____	_____
_____	_____	_____

I'm Thinking

I'm Feeling

I'm Doing

Record your thoughts, feelings and behaviors when experiencing anger on the TFB chart.

Anger Journal

WHAT: What am I angry about? Find your source:

_____

_____

_____

_____

WHO: Who am I angry at? Find your target:

_____

_____

_____

_____

WHEN: When was I angry? Give the date and time:

_____

_____

_____

_____

WHERE: Where did it occur? School, home, social setting etc…:

_____

_____

_____

_____

HOW: How did you resolve it? What was the outcome?

_____

_____

_____

_____

FEELINGS CHART

Which anger style do you have?

SEVEN TOWERS OF ANGER STYLES:

BLAMER: This anger style thinks it is someone else's fault.

EXPLODER: This anger style loses his or her temper and starts yelling, throwing things, hitting and so on.

PUT DOWNER: Gets nasty saying sarcastic or hurtful things.

STUFFER: Holds everything in and pretends like nothing is wrong.

TRIANGULATOR: Gossips and sucks other people into the conflict, trying to get someone to take his or her side.

WITHDRAWER: Pulls out of the situation and quits talking to the person they are angry at.

PROBLEM SOLVER: Can admit when they are wrong and feels the need to fix everyone's situation.

Write down the people in your life that fit each profile:

BLAMER: _____

EXPLODER: _____

PUT DOWNER: _____

STUFFER: _____

TRIANGULATOR: _____

WITHDRAWER: _____

*PROBLEM SOLVER:*_____

For the next 7 days, write down what anger style you became. This activity will help you become aware of how you deal with anger. Awareness is the key to change.

MONDAY: _____

TUESDAY: _____

WEDNESDAY: _____

THURSDAY: _____

FRIDAY: _____

SATURDAY: _____

SUNDAY: _____

ANGER-RESENTMENT-RAGE EXPLODE METER

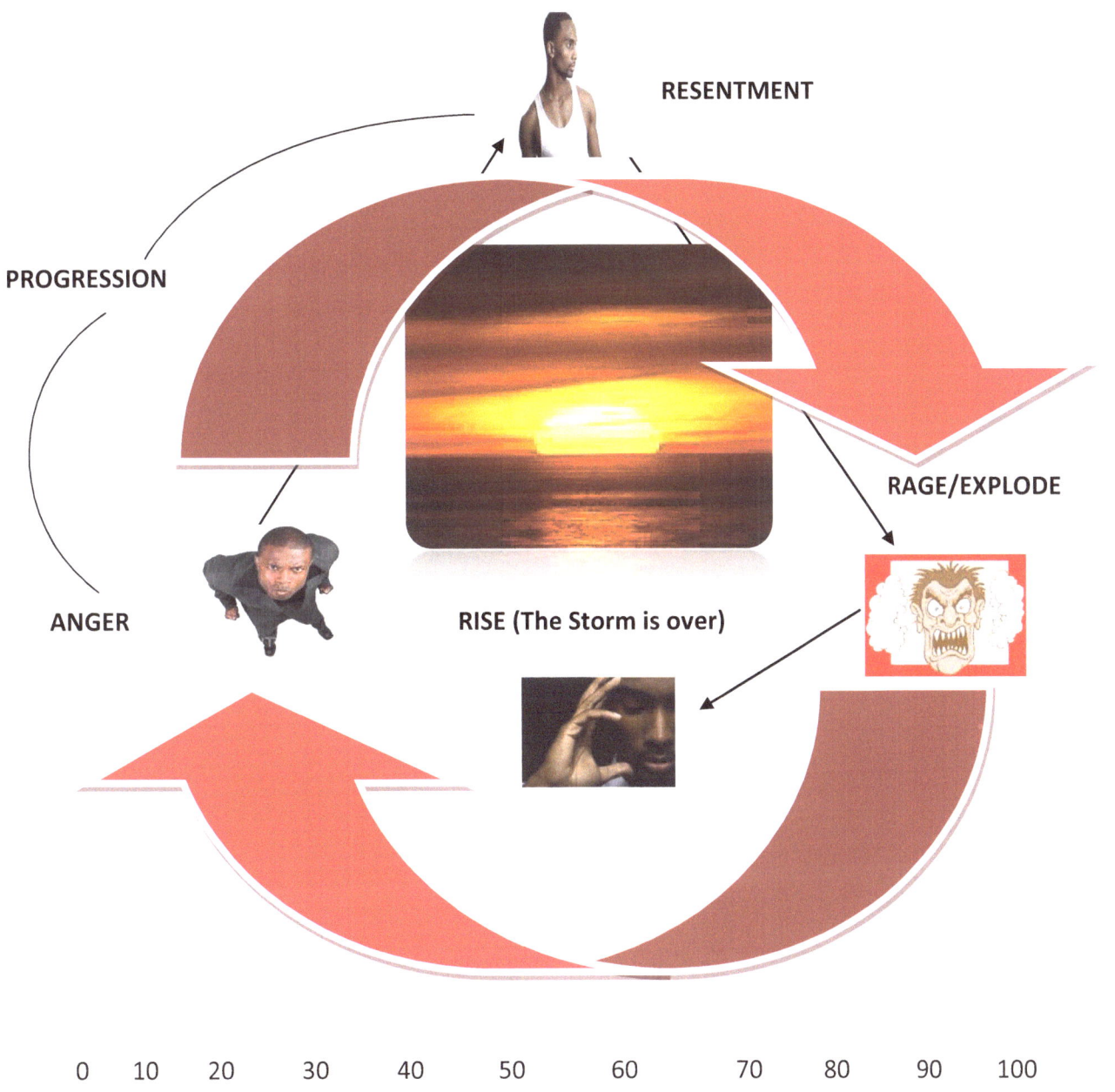

RESENTMENT

PROGRESSION

RAGE/EXPLODE

ANGER

RISE (The Storm is over)

| 0 | 10 | 20 | 30 | 40 | 50 | 60 | 70 | 80 | 90 | 100 |

When anger is not expressed appropriately unresolved anger turns into resentment unresolved resentment turns into rage, which has two components. Component A: Cognitive Movement and Component B: Physical Altercation. When these two components interchange with each other temporary insanity can occur. After this phase you will experience the quiet storm. Here is where you collect your thoughts and examine your behavior.

Where are you on this meter? Chart where you are on a weekly basis.

WEEK 1

Anger: Why?

_____

_____

Resentment: Why?

_____

_____

Rage: Why?

_____

_____

Explode: Why?

_____

_____

RISE: Why?

_____

_____

SELF KNOWLEDGE:

What did you learn from this step?

_____
_____
_____
_____
_____
_____
_____
_____
_____
_____
_____
_____
_____
_____
_____
_____
_____
_____
_____
_____
_____
_____
_____
_____
_____
_____
_____
_____
_____

Week 3

Anger Reduction Plan

This step is powerful because you will learn how to utilize your anger reduction plan. One of the reasons anger is so powerful is because people give it power. Last week you learned about psychosocial stressors that caused anger. This next step will assist you in developing your own anger reduction plan to mitigate your anger and ultimately block the progression so you don't reach the final stage on the ARR meter which is rage.

An effective set of strategies for controlling anger should include both immediate and preventive strategies. Anger reduction is an ongoing process designed to control stemming aggressive thoughts, feelings and behaviors.

I. **The Keys to Anger Management**

Assess your triggers. You'll be better prepared to manage your anger if you know what things are apt to get you.

Notice your signs. Pay attention to your body's anger signs.

Get yourself under control. Give yourself time to stop and think by taking a deep breath, letting your muscles relax, or taking a time-out.

Evaluate your response. Notice what thoughts and feelings are feeding your anger, and what you're getting out of your response.

Read the scene. Decide if you want to walk away or confront the situation.

II. **Five Steps to Taming Anger**

Step 1: know what pushes your **"anger** "buttons you probably could name a few things you've gotten angry about. Maybe the list is pretty long. Think of these as your anger buttons. You get mad when they're pushed.

Step 2: know your body's anger **"warning signs"**. If you pay close attention, your body will tell you when you're getting mad.

Step 3: stop and think. Anger is a tricky emotion. You could even call it a **"master of disguise"**. That's because anger is often a mask that hides another feeling. Anger is sometimes a cover-up for: frustration, fear, sadness, shame, disappointment, jealousy and guilt.

Step 4: cage your rage. Anger is a strong emotion, but you are stronger. You have a choice about how to handle yourself. It takes a strong person to make the right choice……..You can do it.

Step 5: decide what to do. Once you've pulled yourself together, it's time to figure out what to do about what's making you mad. Doing something is important because it means you are taking action. The trick is, don't take a negative action, like hurting someone with your fists or your words. You want to make a good choice, you show anger that you are the boss.

III.   Thought Stopping Technique

You will need to close your eyes and picture a stop sign in your mind, telling you to stop whenever you are experiencing unwanted thoughts.

IV.   Time Out

Time out is only effective when used on a regular basis. Get into the habit of learning your body's cues to guide you in the process of knowing which action to take that will be most effective for you. Time out is essential because it allows you to examine your thoughts and behavior for immediate and preventive strategies for any situation.

Can you think of a situation in which time out would be the most appropriate strategy?

_____

_____

Please describe the strategies that you used to maintain your anger.

_____

_____

V. De-Escalation Technique

THE SIX QUICK WAYS TO CALM DOWN

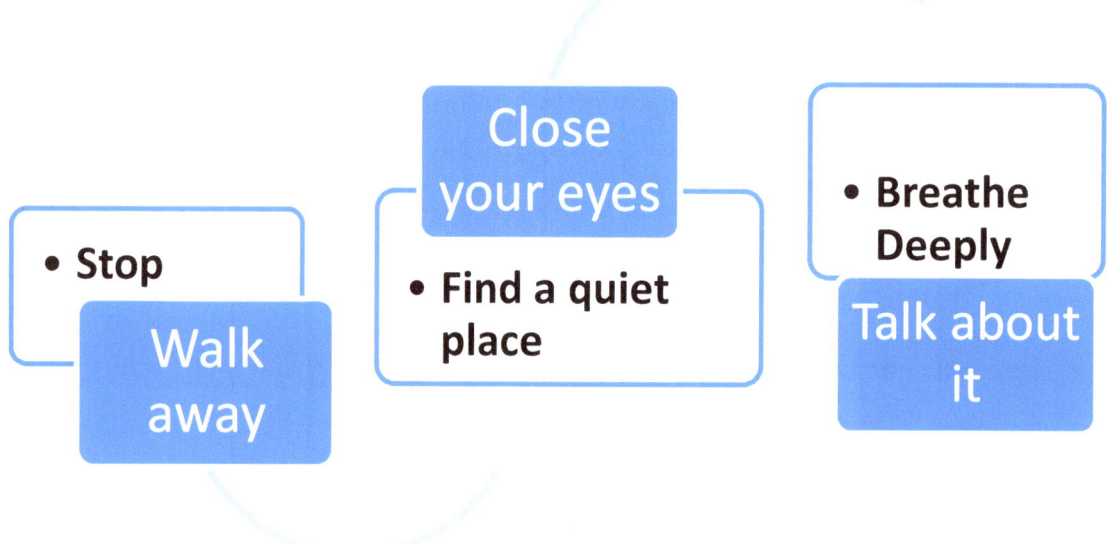

Step 1: Stop: Stop right there in your tracks and envision a stop sign, don't go any further.

Step2: Walk Away: by knowing your triggers, you can avoid getting into confrontational situations by walking away.

Step 3: Find a quiet place: get away from the situation to wherever you find peace. Pay attention to the serene sounds and sights around you.

Step 4: Close your eyes: get into a comfortable position and close your eyes then try to block out your stressors. Ask yourself, what is the best thing that can happen from this situation? Then ask yourself what is the worst thing that can happen.

Step 5: Breathe Deeply: breathing is the foundation of sanity because it provides our brain with the oxygen needed for us to gain our equilibrium.

- *Now breathe in slowly to a count of three*

- *Hold this breath for a count of three.*

- *Exhale slowly for a count of three.*

- *Rest for a count of three, without taking any breathes*

- *Take two normal breathes*

- *Pay attention to your body's reaction and where your thoughts are.*

- *Start this process from the beginning as much as you need*

Whew you needed that!!!!

Step 6: Talk about it: when you are ready, open your eyes and find someone to talk to. Sometimes taking time out allows for a new perspective on the situation.

Now take a look at the situation without judgment, ask yourself:

What really happened here?

_____

_____

How can this experience be feedback?

_____

_____

What can I do differently next time?

_____

_____

VI. Keeping In Touch With My Anger

Where do I see myself on the anger meter?

What were my cues that provoked my anger?

T: _____

F: _____

B: _____

What was the situation that provoked my anger?

_____

_____

What was my response to the situation?

_____

_____

What strategies were effective for me in this situation?

_____

_____

What could I have done differently?

_____

_____

VII. Consequences for Out Of Control Anger

   a) *Loss of employment*
   b) *Incarceration*
   c) *Relationship problems*
   d) *School suspension*

e)   *Fights*

　　　f)   *Loss of friends*

VIII.   Health Risk Factors For Out Of Control Anger

→ *High Blood Pressure*

→ *Head aches*

→*Heart Disease*

→ *Tension*

Anger Journal

WHAT: What am I angry about? Find your source:

_____
_____
_____
_____

WHO: Who am I angry at? Find your target:

_____
_____
_____
_____

WHEN: When was I angry? Give the date and time:

_____
_____
_____
_____

WHERE: Where did it occur? School, home, social setting etc…:

_____
_____
_____
_____

HOW: How did you resolve it? What was the outcome?

_____
_____
_____
_____

FEELINGS CHART

Which anger style do you have?

SEVEN TOWERS OF ANGER STYLES:

BLAMER: *This anger style thinks it is someone else's fault.*

EXPLODER: *This anger style loses his or her temper and starts yelling, throwing things, hitting and so on.*

PUT DOWNER: *Gets nasty saying sarcastic or hurtful things.*

STUFFER: *Holds everything in and pretends like nothing is wrong.*

TRIANGULATOR: *Gossips and sucks other people into the conflict, trying to get someone to take his or her side.*

WITHDRAWER: *Pulls out of the situation and quits talking to the person they are angry at.*

PROBLEM SOLVER: *Can admit when they are wrong and feels the need to fix everyone's situation.*

Write down the people in your life that fit each profile:

BLAMER: _____

EXPLODER: _____

PUT DOWNER: _____

STUFFER: _____

TRIANGULATOR: _____

WITHDRAWER: _____

PROBLEM SOLVER:_____

For the next 7 days, write down what anger style you became. This activity will help you become aware of how you deal with anger. Awareness is the key to change.

MONDAY: _____

TUESDAY: _____

WEDNESDAY: _____

THURSDAY: _____

FRIDAY: _____

SATURDAY: _____

SUNDAY: _____

ANGER-RESENTMENT-RAGE EXPLODE METER

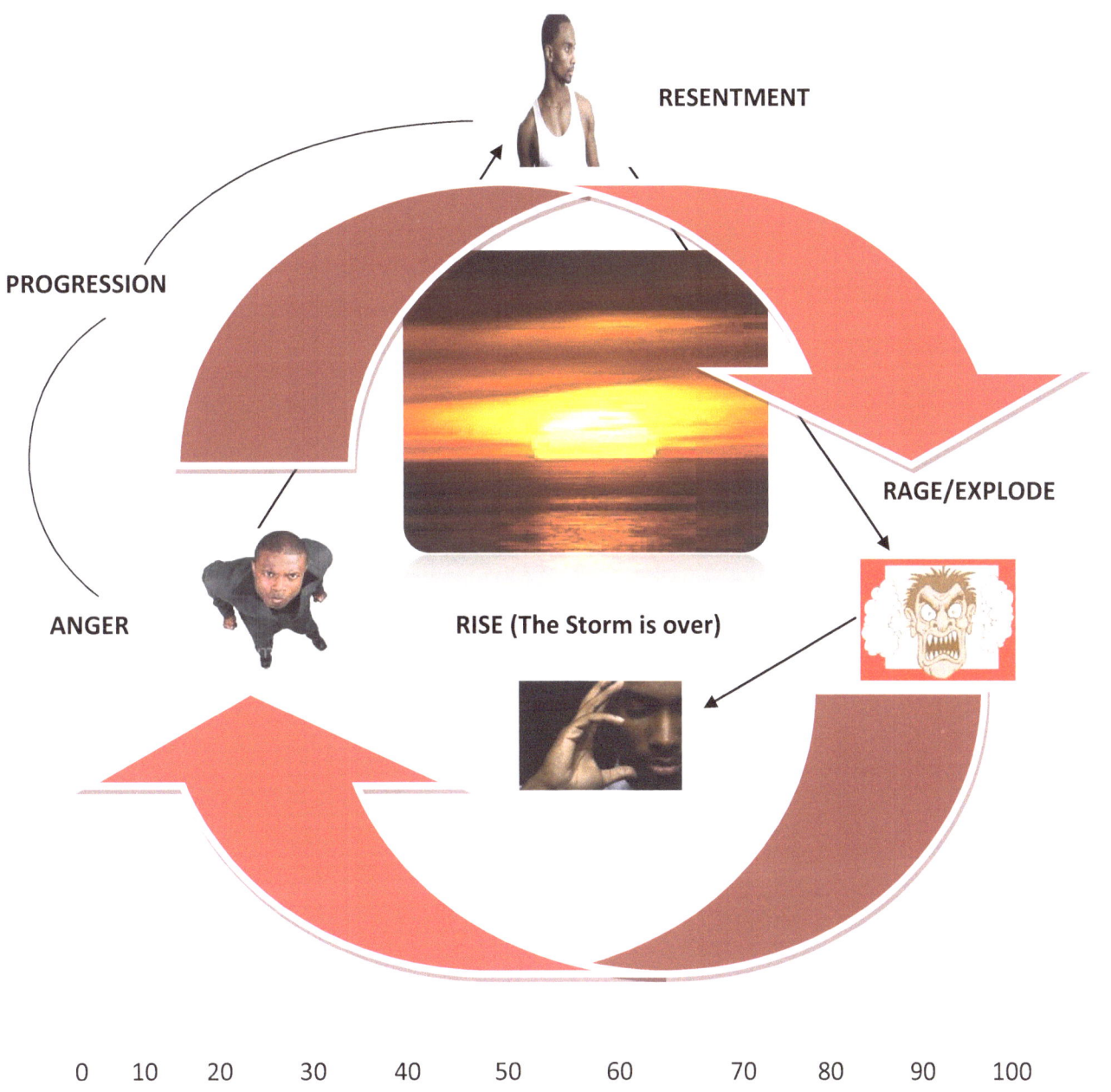

RESENTMENT

PROGRESSION

RAGE/EXPLODE

ANGER

RISE (The Storm is over)

0   10   20   30   40   50   60   70   80   90   100

When anger is not expressed appropriately unresolved anger turns into resentment unresolved resentment turns into rage, which has two components. Component A: Cognitive Movement and Component B: Physical Altercation. When these two components interchange with each other temporary insanity can occur. After this phase you will experience the quiet storm. Here is where you collect your thoughts and examine your behavior.

Where are you on this meter? Chart where you are on a weekly basis.

WEEK 1

Anger: Why?

_____

_____

Resentment: Why?

_____

_____

Rage: Why?

_____

_____

Explode: Why?

_____

_____

RISE: Why?

_____

_____

SELF KNOWLEDGE:

What did you learn from this step?

_____
_____
_____
_____
_____
_____
_____
_____
_____
_____
_____
_____
_____
_____
_____
_____
_____
_____
_____
_____
_____
_____
_____
_____
_____
_____
_____
_____

Week 4

The Choice Is Yours

This step is vital, now is the time to look at the man in the mirror and make that psychological incision and examine your soul, in doing so you now have the opportunity to make a change. You will learn how to explore more deeply the things that maybe blocking you from maintaining your anger.

I.   RISE

The RISE model is helpful in understanding your options which assist you in maintaining your anger.

R-Reflect & Examine: this step provides you with a starting point to begin thinking about your situation and allows you opportunities to examine the options available toward understanding them.

I-Imagine & Intentions: this step encourages you to tap into your imagination to create a vision to assist in developing realistic options and plans to accomplish them.

S-Solutions: this step will assist you to continue to explore in detail the options you listed and the advantages of each one.

E-Evaluate: this step helps you determine if your solutions are realistic and obtainable, if so select an option or options.

NOW RISE! IF YOU CAN LOOK UP, YOU CAN GET UP!!!!

II. RISE Model

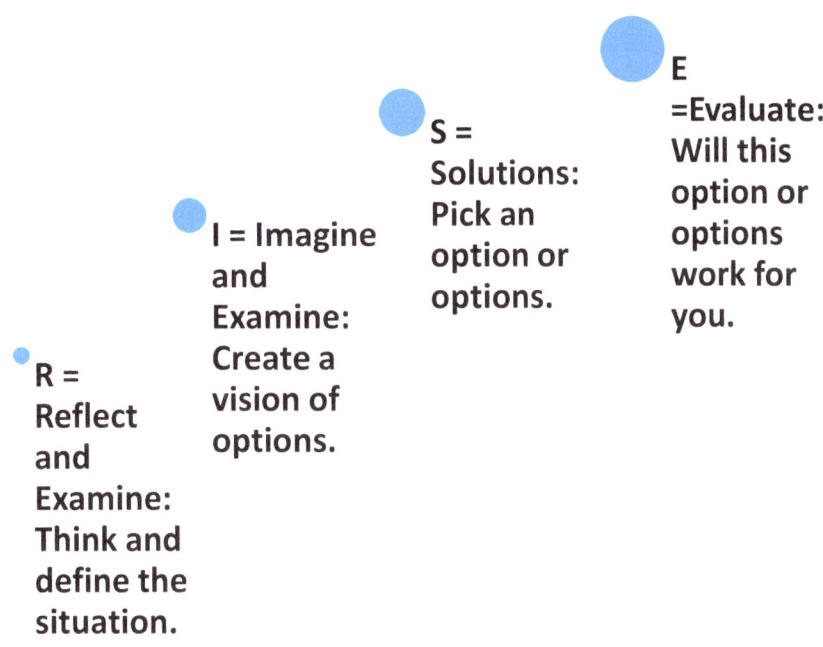

**R =
Reflect
and
Examine:
Think and
define the
situation.**

**I = Imagine
and
Examine:
Create a
vision of
options.**

**S =
Solutions:
Pick an
option or
options.**

**E
=Evaluate:
Will this
option or
options
work for
you.**

III. Reviewing Your Options

One of the primary reasons for using the RISE model is to assist in reaching solutions to any situation you encounter. This can be accomplished by using the RISE Model on a daily basis.

What is the situation I'm dealing with?

_____

_____

What can I do about this situation?

_____

_____

What did I do about this situation?

_____

_____

Did this solution work for me?

_____

_____

Anger Journal

WHAT: What am I angry about? Find your source:

_____

_____

_____

_____

WHO: Who am I angry at? Find your target:

_____

_____

_____

_____

WHEN: When was I angry? Give the date and time:

_____

_____

_____

_____

WHERE: Where did it occur? School, home, social setting etc…:

_____

_____

_____

_____

HOW: How did you resolve it? What was the outcome?

_____

_____

_____

_____

FEELINGS CHART

Which anger style do you have?

SEVEN TOWERS OF ANGER STYLES:

BLAMER: *This anger style thinks it is someone else's fault.*

EXPLODER: *This anger style loses his or her temper and starts yelling, throwing things, hitting and so on.*

PUT DOWNER: *Gets nasty saying sarcastic or hurtful things.*

STUFFER: *Holds everything in and pretends like nothing is wrong.*

TRIANGULATOR: *Gossips and sucks other people into the conflict, trying to get someone to take his or her side.*

WITHDRAWER: *Pulls out of the situation and quits talking to the person they are angry at.*

PROBLEM SOLVER: *Can admit when they are wrong and feels the need to fix everyone's situation.*

Write down the people in your life that fit each profile:

BLAMER: _____

EXPLODER: _____

PUT DOWNER: _____

STUFFER: _____

TRIANGULATOR: _____

WITHDRAWER: _____

PROBLEM SOLVER: _____

For the next 7 days, write down what anger style you became. This activity will help you become aware of how you deal with anger. Awareness is the key to change.

MONDAY: _____

TUESDAY: _____

WEDNESDAY: _____

THURSDAY: _____

FRIDAY: _____

SATURDAY: _____

SUNDAY: _____

ANGER-RESENTMENT-RAGE EXPLODE METER

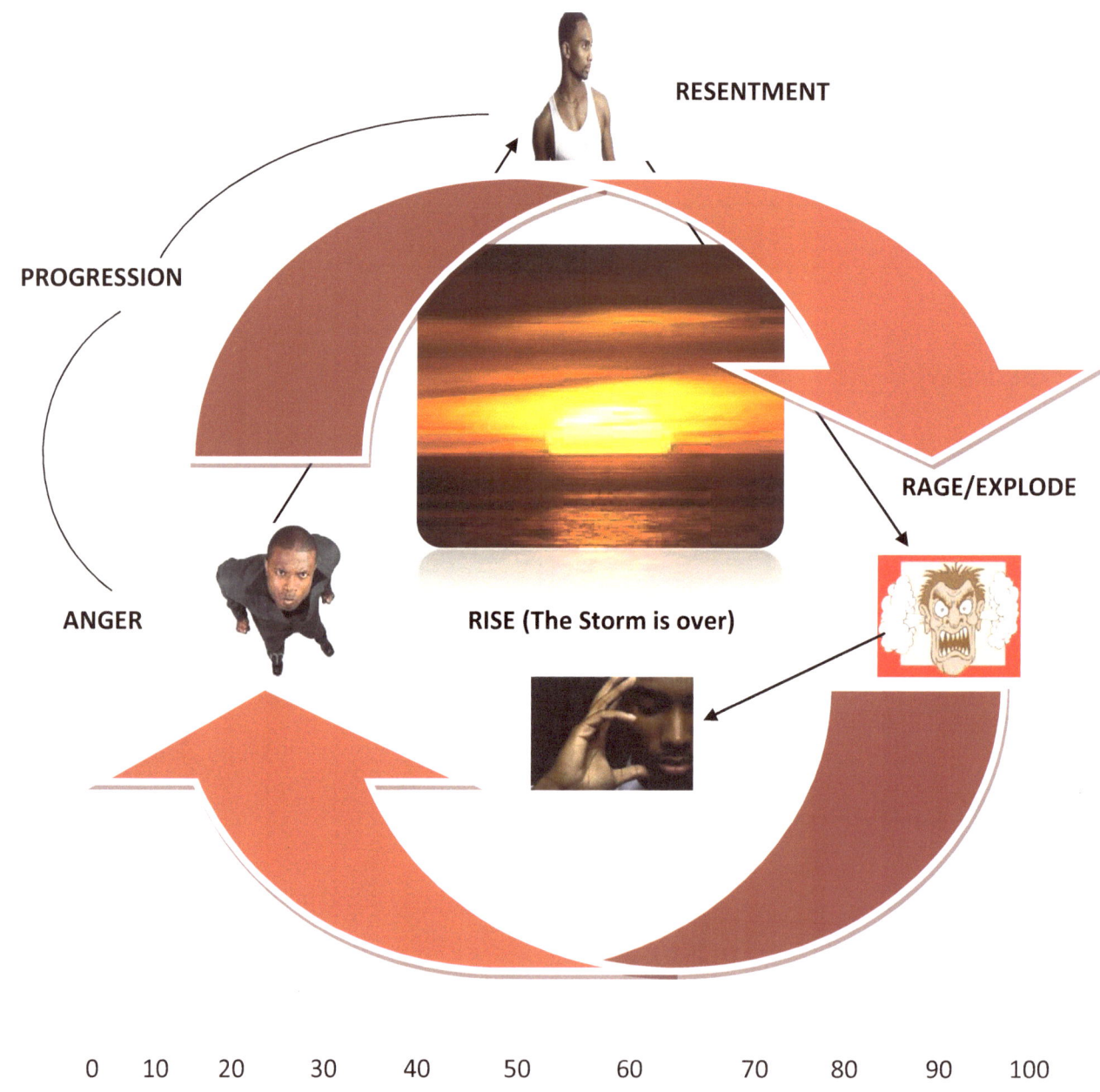

RESENTMENT

PROGRESSION

RAGE/EXPLODE

ANGER

RISE (The Storm is over)

0   10   20   30   40   50   60   70   80   90   100

When anger is not expressed appropriately unresolved anger turns into resentment unresolved resentment turns into rage, which has two components. Component A: Cognitive Movement and Component B: Physical Altercation. When these two components interchange with each other temporary insanity can occur. After this phase you will experience the quiet storm. Here is where you collect your thoughts and examine your behavior.

Where are you on this meter? Chart where you are on a weekly basis.

WEEK 1

Anger: Why?

_____
_____

Resentment: Why?

_____
_____

Rage: Why?

_____
_____

Explode: Why?

_____
_____

RISE: Why?

_____
_____

SELF KNOWLEDGE:

What did you learn from this step?

_____
_____
_____
_____
_____
_____
_____
_____
_____
_____
_____
_____
_____
_____
_____
_____
_____
_____
_____
_____
_____
_____
_____
_____
_____
_____
_____
_____
_____

Week 5

Balancing You

This section is one of if not the most important section in this workbook. Balancing you encompasses just that, the holistic self. We've talked about stopping the manifestations of anger, anger reduction plan, and the choice is yours. Balancing you brings it all together to give you a more complete picture of what it takes to become and maintain your anger.

I.   *Balancing You*

Can African American males live a balanced life? Can they man- up and experience the power of their emotions at the same time? It is very crucial for the African American male to be spiritual, mental and physically healthy to make the adjustments in the areas of their lives that is slowly and silently killing them. Having a spiritual, mental and physical balance is the key to life.

What messages did you receive as a young African American male pertaining to becoming a man?

_____
_____
_____

Have you ever been told that African American males do not express their feelings or emotions such as: males do not cry? If so, who expressed that to you?

_____
_____
_____

What were the values you learned while growing up as an African American male? Who taught you these values?

_____
_____
_____

During your developmental stages were there things you were taught about being an African American male that you now question?

_____
_____
_____

Based on your own experiences of being an African American male, what does this mean to you?

_____
_____
_____

II.　　Relationships

African American males do not hold their respected place in relationships today for reasons that go very deep. It must be a place where each individual regards the other person's rights and feelings as they would their own. This is a crucial element that is missing in the majority of African American relationships. African American males have trouble bonding because if the father is not present in the home, they do not have the opportunity to see their parents bond. Many grow up like a flower deprived of sunshine and water. Some are robbed of spiritual, psychological, emotional and intellectual growth because the father is not there to give the male parental instruction. Without this vital instruction the young African American male has nothing to mimic from.

Describe your relationships with others:

_____
_____

Identify factors that contribute to having a healthy relationship:

_____
_____

What is your understanding of how to develop healthy relationships?

_____

_____

III.   Human Sexuality

You've been told that "Men are from Mars and Women are from Venus". What this entails is that women look at sex indirectly and men look at it directly. Women value intimacy directly and men value intimacy indirectly. When there's a distortion in this concept African American men become angry. African American men have been taught not to feel or express their emotions in an open manner. Only during sex do men feel they have permission to express their dominance.

Did you ever experience anger when your girlfriend refused to have sex? Yes__

No__

Did you ever experience anger when your girlfriend refused to perform specific sexual acts? Yes___ No___

If you experienced anger how did you handle it? Please explain?

_____

_____

_____

IV.   Drugs and Alcohol

African American males often turn to drugs and alcohol. This generic process is used by African American males to anesthetize their internal conflict. This erases the degrading and cruel treatment that they feel society has dealt them. African American males need to know that selling, taking drugs and drinking alcohol does not solve their problems. Matter of fact, alcohol and drugs magnifies their internal conflict that produces anger.

Do you recall ever showing anger under the influence of alcohol or drugs? Yes___ No___

If yes, please explain:

_____

_____

_____

V.   Crime and Violence

Many African American males engage in crimes because of their lack of economic resources. However, this is not an excuse to participate in unlawful behaviors. Where do they learn this behavior from? One reason could be that they do not have visual positive African American role models. The most visual role models that they encounter are pimps, players, cons, hustler's and drug dealers. This type of observation feeds into criminal behavior that ultimately produces violence.

Have you ever committed a crime and found yourself feeling angry? Yes___ No___

If yes, please explain:

_____

_____

_____

VI.   Creative Problem Solving

This is an area where you can determine what methods or models worked for you. Commit them to memory and practice, practice, practice.

Which model or method worked best for you? Please explain:

_____

_____

_____

Anger Journal

WHAT: What am I angry about? Find your source:

_____
_____
_____
_____

WHO: Who am I angry at? Find your target:

_____
_____
_____
_____

WHEN: When was I angry? Give the date and time:

_____
_____
_____
_____

WHERE: Where did it occur? School, home, social setting etc…:

_____
_____
_____
_____

HOW: How did you resolve it? What was the outcome?

_____
_____
_____
_____
_____

FEELINGS CHART

Which anger style do you have?

SEVEN TOWERS OF ANGER STYLES:

BLAMER: *This anger style thinks it is someone else's fault.*

EXPLODER: *This anger style loses his or her temper and starts yelling, throwing things, hitting and so on.*

PUT DOWNER: *Gets nasty saying sarcastic or hurtful things.*

STUFFER: *Holds everything in and pretends like nothing is wrong.*

TRIANGULATOR: *Gossips and sucks other people into the conflict, trying to get someone to take his or her side.*

WITHDRAWER: *Pulls out of the situation and quits talking to the person they are angry at.*

PROBLEM SOLVER: *Can admit when they are wrong and feels the need to fix everyone's situation.*

Write down the people in your life that fit each profile:

BLAMER: _____

EXPLODER: _____

PUT DOWNER: _____

STUFFER: _____

TRIANGULATOR: _____

WITHDRAWER: _____

PROBLEM SOLVER: _____

For the next 7 days, write down what anger style you became. This activity will help you become aware of how you deal with anger. Awareness is the key to change.

MONDAY: _____

TUESDAY: _____

WEDNESDAY: _____

THURSDAY: _____

FRIDAY: _____

SATURDAY: _____

SUNDAY: _____

ANGER-RESENTMENT-RAGE EXPLODE METER

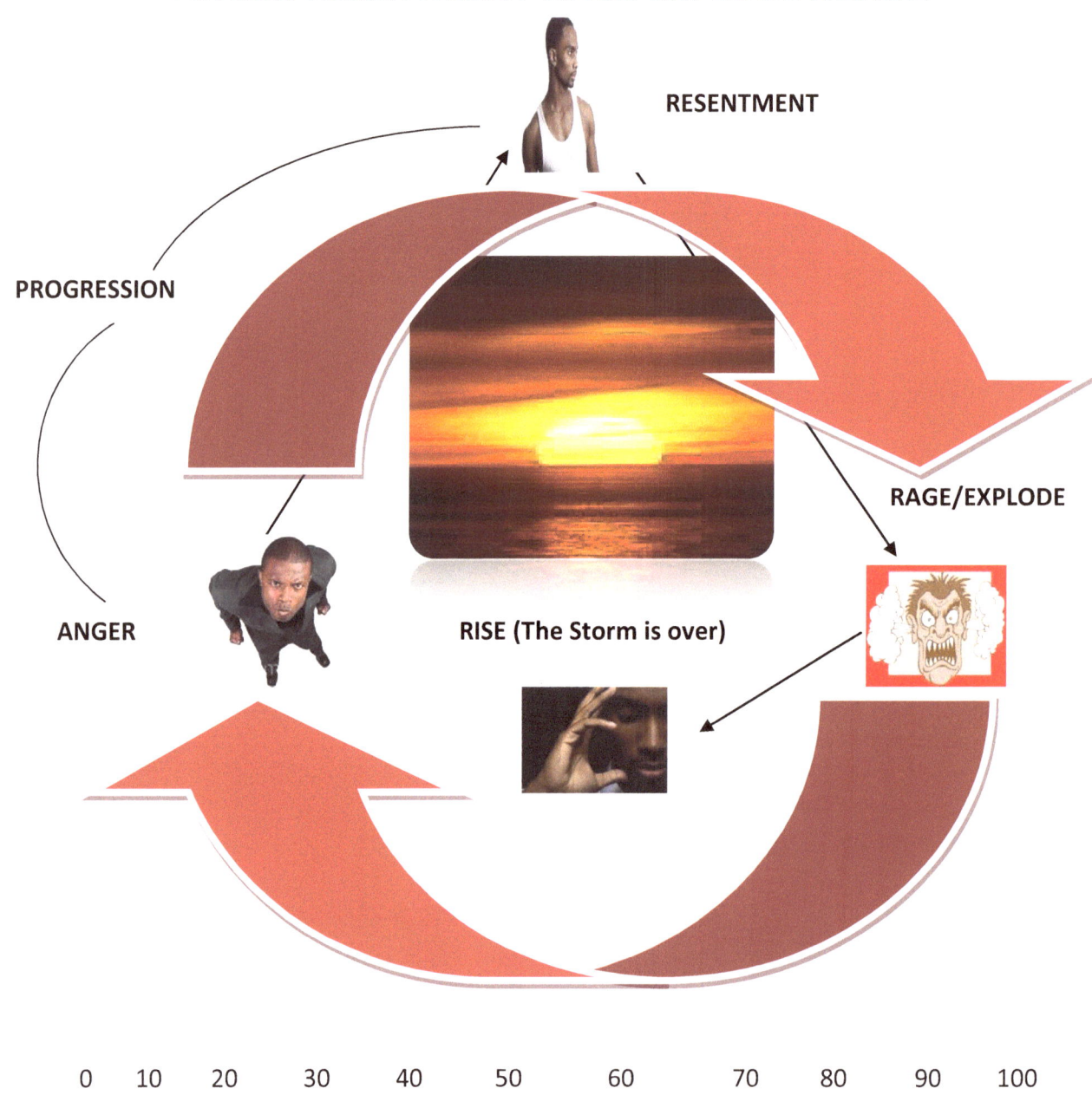

RESENTMENT

PROGRESSION

RAGE/EXPLODE

ANGER

RISE (The Storm is over)

0   10   20   30   40   50   60   70   80   90   100

When anger is not expressed appropriately unresolved anger turns into resentment unresolved resentment turns into rage, which has two components. Component A: Cognitive Movement and Component B: Physical Altercation. When these two components interchange with each other temporary insanity can occur. After this phase you will experience the quiet storm. Here is where you collect your thoughts and examine your behavior.

Where are you on this meter? Chart where you are on a weekly basis.

WEEK 1

Anger: Why?

_____

_____

Resentment: Why?

_____

_____

Rage: Why?

_____

_____

Explode: Why?

_____

_____

RISE: Why?

_____

_____

SELF KNOWLEDGE:

What did you learn from this step?

_____
_____
_____
_____
_____
_____
_____
_____
_____
_____
_____
_____
_____
_____
_____
_____
_____
_____
_____
_____
_____
_____
_____
_____
_____
_____
_____
_____
_____
_____

Week 6

The Manifestation of Anger

Most African American males see anger as a bad thing. It can definitely get us into trouble if we do not handle it well. But anger can also be a gift. Anger is one of our greatest motivators in terms of making important changes. On the other hand, anger can be our greatest enemy. Anger is an emotion that affects all human beings, and the key is what you do with it. Young African American males are having serious problems handling their anger. This may explain why young African American males are dying from lead poisoning (shooting each other).

I.   Four Ways to Understanding The Manifestation of Anger

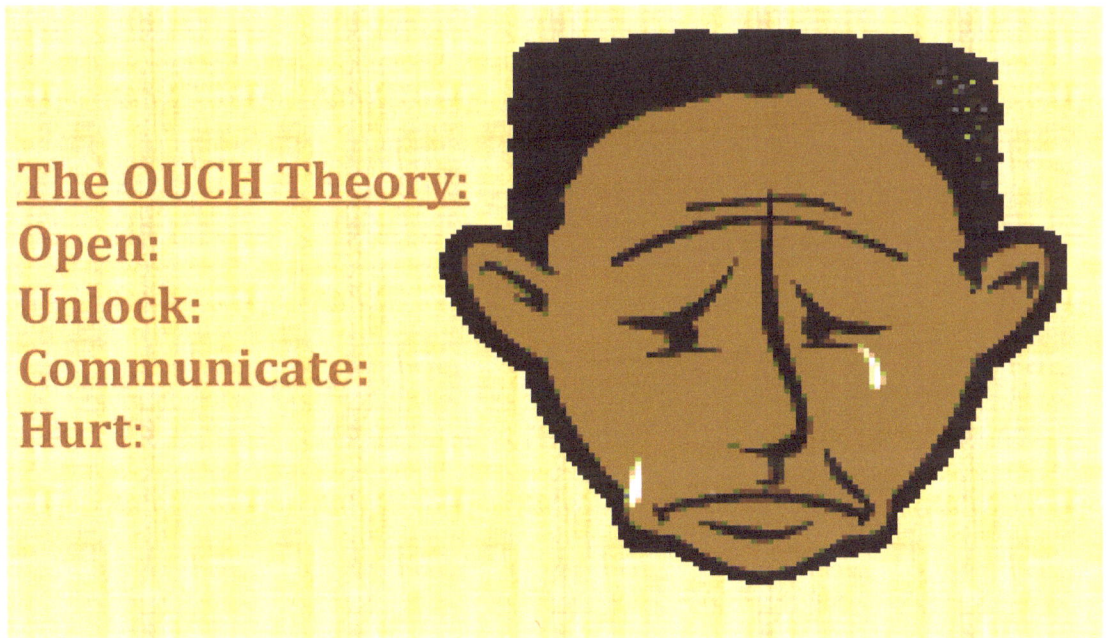

The OUCH Theory:
Open:
Unlock:
Communicate:
Hurt:

The OUCH Theory:

Open: up your mind by using the cause and effect theory. For every action there is a reaction.

Unlock: suppressed feelings. Letting go of these feelings, start you on your path for healing the pains of anger.

Communicate: talk to someone about your feelings and emotions of anger.

Hurt: occurs when there is a direct blow to your morals, values and belief system. Express the hurt you've experienced by using positive behaviors.

II.   Anger

Anger appears to be the African American male's greatest downfall because they do not handle it well. They tend to allow their pride and ego to battle with each other that ultimately causes serious internal conflict. Anger develops when an individual has a distorted perception either audio or visual toward the opposition.

III.   Resentment

Resentment occurs when anger is unresolved. Resentment is the aftermath of anger. This happens when an individual is uncomfortable being around the person that initiated the anger. If resentment is unresolved it will lay dormant and eventually surface as rage.

IV.   Rage

This phase of the manifestation of anger can be fatal. Rage is a behavioral outburst. When an individual reaches this stage of rage they will experience two phases: Cognitive Movement and Physical Altercation.

Cognitive Movement: occurs when an individual is thinking about what they are going to do to someone if they don't stop bothering them.

Physical Altercation: occurs when an individual can no longer tolerate the behavior by the opposition and explode into temporary insanity, in which has a duration of 7seconds. Immediately after the physical altercation phase the individual will experience the **"quiet storm phase"**. This phase is where the individual becomes shame based and needs 50 feet to gather their thoughts about what just happened.

Write down your manifestation of anger and show how your anger progressed?

What sparked your anger?

_____
_____
_____

How did you handle your resentment?

_____
_____
_____

What were you thinking about when the person that you were angry at continued to bother you?

_____
_____
_____

How did you release your anger?

_____
_____
_____

What happened after you released your anger?

_____
_____
_____

Anger Journal

WHAT: What am I angry about? Find your source:

_____
_____
_____
_____

WHO: Who am I angry at? Find your target:

_____
_____
_____
_____

WHEN: When was I angry? Give the date and time:

_____
_____
_____
_____

WHERE: Where did it occur? School, home, social setting etc…:

_____
_____
_____
_____

HOW: How did you resolve it? What was the outcome?

_____
_____
_____
_____
_____

FEELINGS CHART

Which anger style do you have?

SEVEN TOWERS OF ANGER STYLES:

BLAMER: *This anger style thinks it is someone else's fault.*

EXPLODER: *This anger style loses his or her temper and starts yelling, throwing things, hitting and so on.*

PUT DOWNER: *Gets nasty saying sarcastic or hurtful things.*

STUFFER: *Holds everything in and pretends like nothing is wrong.*

TRIANGULATOR: *Gossips and sucks other people into the conflict, trying to get someone to take his or her side.*

WITHDRAWER: *Pulls out of the situation and quits talking to the person they are angry at.*

PROBLEM SOLVER: *Can admit when they are wrong and feels the need to fix everyone's situation.*

Write down the people in your life that fit each profile:

BLAMER: _____

EXPLODER: _____

PUT DOWNER: _____

STUFFER: _____

TRIANGULATOR: _____

WITHDRAWER: _____

PROBLEM SOLVER:_____

For the next 7 days, write down what anger style you became. This activity will help you become aware of how you deal with anger. Awareness is the key to change.

MONDAY: _____

TUESDAY: _____

WEDNESDAY: _____

THURSDAY: _____

FRIDAY: _____

SATURDAY: _____

SUNDAY: _____

ANGER-RESENTMENT-RAGE EXPLODE METER

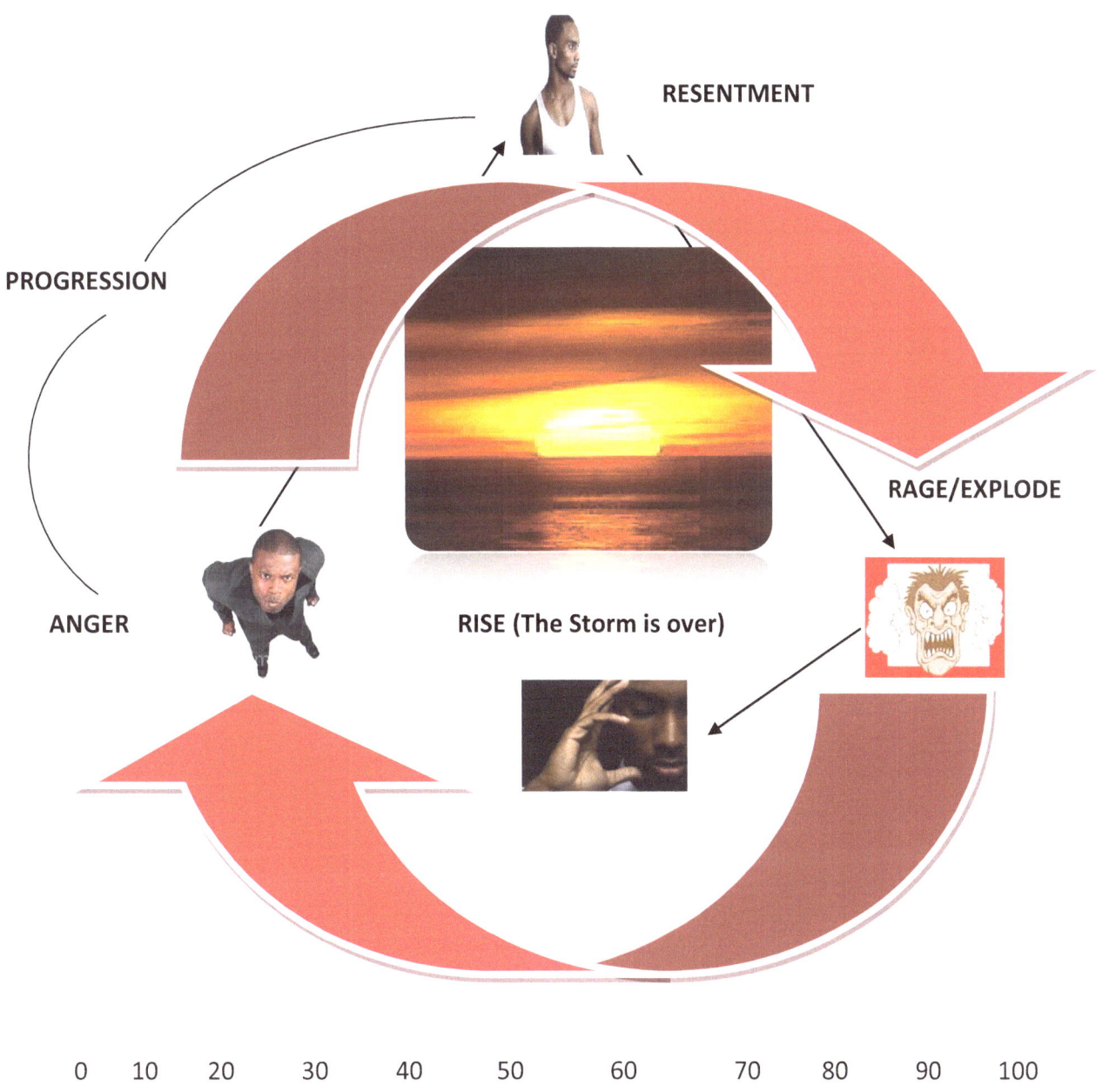

RESENTMENT

PROGRESSION

RAGE/EXPLODE

ANGER

RISE (The Storm is over)

0   10   20   30   40   50   60   70   80   90   100

When anger is not expressed appropriately unresolved anger turns into resentment unresolved resentment turns into rage, which has two components. Component A: Cognitive Movement and Component B: Physical Altercation. When these two components interchange with each other temporary insanity can occur. After this phase you will experience the quiet storm. Here is where you collect your thoughts and examine your behavior.

Where are you on this meter? Chart where you are on a weekly basis.

WEEK 1

Anger: Why?

_____

_____

Resentment: Why?

_____

_____

Rage: Why?

_____

_____

Explode: Why?

_____

_____

RISE: Why?

_____

_____

SELF KNOWLEDGE:

What did you learn from this step?

_____
_____
_____
_____
_____
_____
_____
_____
_____
_____
_____
_____
_____
_____
_____
_____
_____
_____
_____
_____
_____
_____
_____
_____
_____
_____
_____
_____
_____

Week 7

Do Social Stressors Produce Specific Perceptions?

In this section you will review and summarize the basic concepts of the Stop, Drop and Walk anger management program. If you have any questions pertaining to the clarity and validity of this workbook feel free to ask questions.

I.   Perceptions

Perceptions are the key phrase to anger management. Why? Because the environment is not stressful it is how we learn to perceive it. So, if this is true, we create our own anger by the way we look at a situation. Many African American males' perceptions are distorted by a defunct ego and pride system. Due to this spiritual deficiency young African American males are walking around in a zombie like state, which could possibly leave them permanently scared. If their distorted perceptions remain untreated they will ultimately continue to commit culture genocide.

Have you ever thought that you heard something negative pertaining to you, but later discovered that it was not, if so did you get angry and what did you do about it?

_____

_____

_____

Have you ever saw something or someone and mistakenly identified them as someone that you were angry at, if so did you get angry and what did you do about it?

_____

_____

_____

II.   Closing Notes:

Remember that anger can be (but does not have to be) diabolical. Therefore it is vital that you know and understand that no one wins when you respond negatively to anger. Lastly, when experiencing severe rage the equation to rage is the cemetery or the penitentiary.

Anger Journal

WHAT: What am I angry about? Find your source:

_____
_____
_____
_____

WHO: Who am I angry at? Find your target:

_____
_____
_____
_____

WHEN: When was I angry? Give the date and time:

_____
_____
_____
_____

WHERE: Where did it occur? School, home, social setting etc…:

_____
_____
_____
_____

HOW: How did you resolve it? What was the outcome?

_____
_____
_____
_____
_____

FEELINGS CHART

Which anger style do you have?

SEVEN TOWERS OF ANGER STYLES:

BLAMER: This anger style thinks it is someone else's fault.

EXPLODER: This anger style loses his or her temper and starts yelling, throwing things, hitting and so on.

PUT DOWNER: Gets nasty saying sarcastic or hurtful things.

STUFFER: Holds everything in and pretends like nothing is wrong.

TRIANGULATOR: Gossips and sucks other people into the conflict, trying to get someone to take his or her side.

WITHDRAWER: Pulls out of the situation and quits talking to the person they are angry at.

PROBLEM SOLVER: Can admit when they are wrong and feels the need to fix everyone's situation.

Write down the people in your life that fit each profile:

BLAMER: _____

EXPLODER: _____

PUT DOWNER: _____

STUFFER: _____

TRIANGULATOR: _____

WITHDRAWER: _____

PROBLEM SOLVER: _____

For the next 7 days, write down what anger style you became. This activity will help you become aware of how you deal with anger. Awareness is the key to change.

MONDAY: _____

TUESDAY: _____

WEDNESDAY: _____

THURSDAY: _____

FRIDAY: _____

SATURDAY: _____

SUNDAY: _____

ANGER-RESENTMENT-RAGE EXPLODE METER

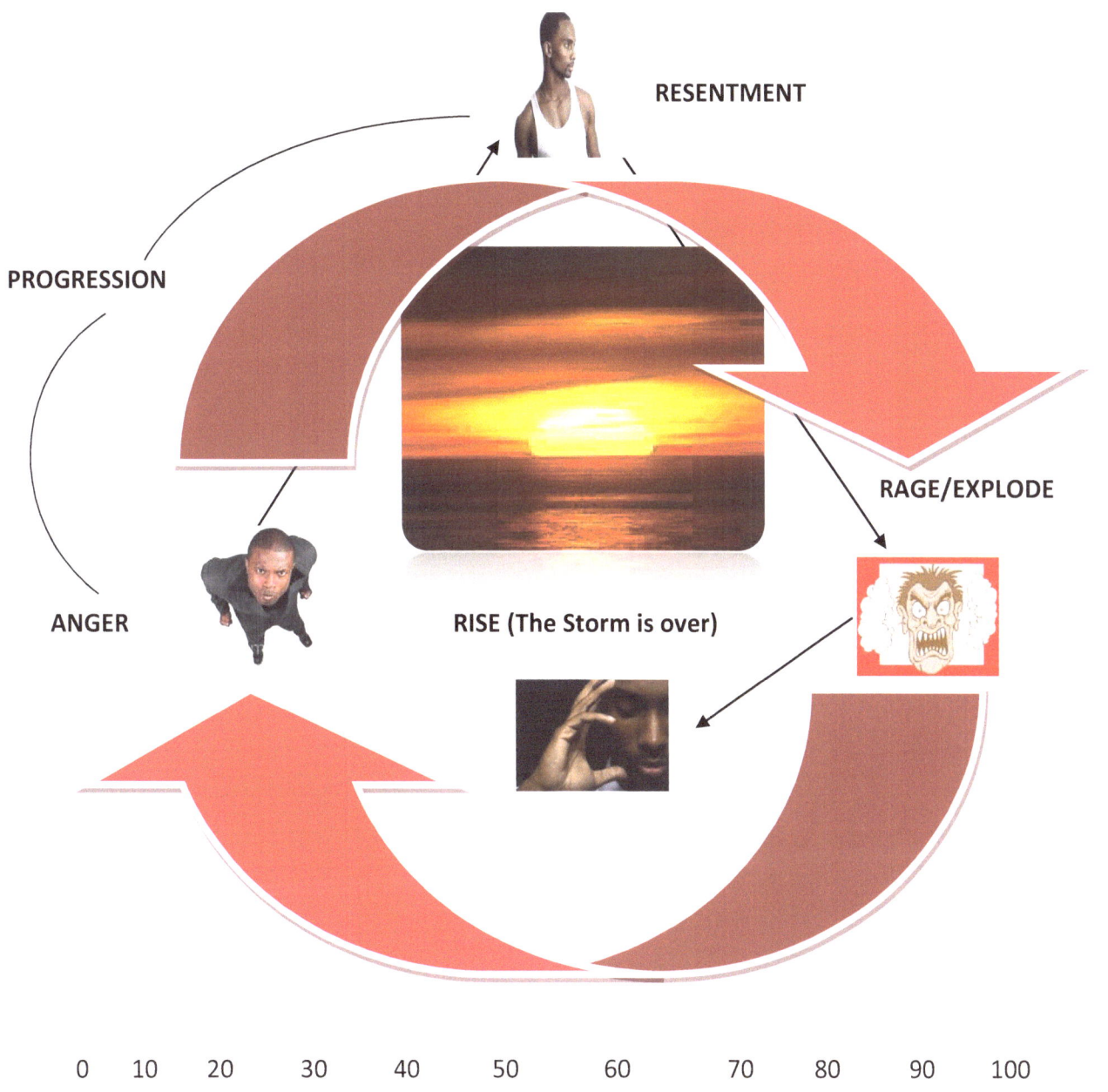

RESENTMENT

PROGRESSION

RAGE/EXPLODE

ANGER

RISE (The Storm is over)

0   10   20   30   40   50   60   70   80   90   100

When anger is not expressed appropriately unresolved anger turns into resentment unresolved resentment turns into rage, which has two components. Component A: Cognitive Movement and Component B: Physical Altercation. When these two components interchange with each other temporary insanity can occur. After this phase you will experience the quiet storm. Here is where you collect your thoughts and examine your behavior.

Where are you on this meter? Chart where you are on a weekly basis.

WEEK 1

Anger: Why?

_____

_____

Resentment: Why?

_____

_____

Rage: Why?

_____

_____

Explode: Why?

_____

_____

RISE: Why?

_____

_____

SELF KNOWLEDGE:

What did you learn from this step?

_____

_____

_____

_____

_____

_____

_____

_____

_____

_____

_____

_____

_____

_____

_____

_____

_____

_____

_____

_____

_____

_____

_____

_____

_____

_____

_____

Week 8 (It's A Wrap)

Have You Modified Your Anger?

In this last session, you will review what you have learned about the Stop Drop and Walk anger management program. You will complete a final questionnaire which measures the knowledge you gained throughout this program.

Self-Awareness

What is anger?

_____

_____

_____

Name 5 Physiological signs of anger:

_____

_____

_____

Why do African American males get angry?

_____

_____

_____

Name 2 relaxation techniques:

_____

_____

_____

What are the steps to anger reduction?

_____

_____

_____

Name 3 consequences for out of control anger:

_____

_____

_____

Name 2 major health risk factors for out of control anger?

_____

_____

_____

Is it ok to become angry? Yes_____ No _____ please explain:

_____

_____

_____

What is the process for effectively using the "Thought Stopping Technique"?

_____

_____

_____

What is the difference between anger, aggression and rage?

_____

_____

_____

Describe and explain your understanding of the RISE Model:

_____

_____

_____

Describe and explain the OUCH Theory:

_____

_____

_____

KEY POINTS TO ANGER

Anger is a normal and necessary emotion.

It is not wrong to experience feelings of anger.

Everyone experiences feelings of anger; some experience it more often and intensely than others.

Anger is your body's way of telling you that something is wrong. It is your body's response to an unmet need, expectation or belief.

Anger can feel wrong to some people because they have been taught that feeling/expressing anger is not good.

Anger can appear wrong when people express it in inappropriate ways, such as using violence.

When expressed appropriately, anger can lead to having your needs met, without hindering the needs of others.

Appropriate expressions of anger can lead to stronger relationships and more satisfying situation.

SELF KNOWLEDGE:

What did you learn from this step?

_____
_____
_____
_____
_____
_____
_____
_____
_____
_____
_____
_____
_____
_____
_____
_____
_____
_____
_____
_____
_____
_____
_____
_____
_____
_____
_____
_____
_____
_____

Write a letter to someone that you have hurt by showing inappropriate anger:

_____

_____

_____

_____

_____

_____

_____

_____

_____

_____

_____

_____

_____

_____

_____

_____

_____

_____

_____

_____

_____

_____

_____

_____

You are now in charge of your anger. YOU GO BOY!

Selected References

Caring for Myself (2010). Lesson 4: Managing Anger. *Retrieved May 21, 2010* , from
        http://www.fcs.msue.msu.edu.

Irving, M. &. (2008). Cultural Identification and Academic Achievement among African American
        males. *Journal of Adavanced Academics 19* , 676-698.

July II, W. (1999). *Understanding The Tin Man: Why So Many Men Avoid Intimacy.* New York:
        DoubleDay.

Microsoft Office Professional. *(2007). Microsoft Office*
        Online ClipArt/Bing selected images and graphics. Redmond, WA: Microsoft
        Corporation One Microsoft Way

Pearson, Y. (2001). Anger Management: *Youth Life Skills. Center City Minnesota: Hazelden*

Reilly PM, Shopshire MS, Durazzo TC, and Campbell TA. *Anger Management for Substance Abuse*
        And Mental Health Clients: Participant Workbook. DHHS Pub. No. (SMA) 03-3817.
        Rockville, MD: Center for Substance Abuse Treatment, Substance Abuse and Mental
        Health Services Administration, reprinted 2003

Stanton, C. (2006). Life Coach in a Box. *Life Coach in a Box* . San Francisco, CA, USA: Chronical
        Books.

William Dr, C. C. (1995). U S Socialeconomic and racial differences in health: patterns and
        explanations.   *Ann Rev Sociology 21* , 349-386.